bush
PUBLISHING
& associates

AMAZING FUTURE

*Your Best Years
Are Ahead of You*

By Samuel Martinez

All scripture quotations, unless otherwise noted, are from the *New King James Version*. Copyright © 1982 by Thomas Nelson Inc. Used by Permission. All rights reserved.

Scripture quotations marked AMP are taken from the *Amplified Bible*. Copyright © 1954, 1958, 1962, 1964, 1965, 1987 By the Lockman Foundation. Used by permission. (www.Lockman.org)

Copyright © 2016 Samuel Martinez

Amazing Love Ministries
216 S. Citrus St. P.O. BOX 503
West Covina Calif. 91791

Bush Publishing & Associates books may be ordered at www.BushPublishing.com or www.Amazon.com.
For further information, please contact:
Bush Publishing & Associates
www.BushPublishing.com

ISBN-13: 978-1-944566-17-3

All rights reserved. No part of this book shall be reproduced, stored in a retrieval system, or transmitted by any means, electronic, mechanical, photocopying, recording, or otherwise, without written permission from the publisher.

Contents

Introduction		3
1	Moses - From Leading Sheep to Leading People	5
2	Joseph - From Papa to Prison	7
3	Joseph - From Bad to Worse to Prime Minister	9
4	Ephraim and Manasseh – So Fruitful You Forget	11
5	Caleb – So Close and Yet so Far	13
6	A Few Do Not's and Do's on Your Way to Your Amazing Future	15
7	Job	17
8	Peter	19
9.	Jesus	21
10	The Apostle John	23
11	The Prodigal's Father	25
12	The Woman in John Chapter 8	27
13	King David	29

14	Finish Your Race	31
15	Your Best Years Are Ahead of You	33
16	What More Shall I Say?	35
17	The Birth of Modern Israel	37
18	The Two Men on the Road to Emmaus	39
19	The People Touched by Jesus' Miracles	43
20	Woman at the Well, John Chapter Four	47
21	The Value of One, The Found Sheep	49
22	The Apostle Paul	53
23	Absent from the Body	57
24	Elijah and the Widow	61
25	Elisha and the Widow	65
26	The Blind Man of John Chapter Nine	69
27	He Lifts You Up	73

Epilogue to Pastors and Others	77
Confession for Your Future	79
Quotations on Your Future	81
Psalms, Hymns, and Spiritual Songs	83
Amazing Love Ministries	87
About the Author	89

Dedication

To Magdalena Garcia, my mother, who taught me the value of always performing with excellence, no matter what I was doing. Love you, Mom.

To Helen McLeod, my friend and secretary, who spent hours proofreading this work. Without her this devotional could not have been completed.

And to all my friends over 80 and 90 years old, who keep blessing and encouraging others and doing what God has called them to do. They are not getting older, only wiser and sweeter. They are living examples of the grace and goodness of God and that our best years are always in front of us.

Introduction

I will make you inhabited as in former times, and do better for you than at your beginnings

Ezekiel 36:11

Your best years are ahead of you. The words to a song say, "You may be down, but it's only the first round. You will be up again." It does not matter to God where you are or what situation you may be in today. I have good news for you. Your best days are ahead of you.

When God met Moses in the burning bush He told him, in essence, "Moses your best years are ahead of you. I have a job for you." Moses probably thought, God I was Prince of Egypt once. I was in the palace of Pharaoh daily. I had great wealth and now I am just a shepherd. On top of that, I can't even talk right. Oh, and did you forget, God, I am eighty years old? Eighty. I have hit the big 8-0! My best years just passed me by. But did God listen? No, because God always sees our future when we only tend to see our past. The next forty years were the best years of Moses' life.

The best years of your marriage are ahead of you. The best years of your relationship with your children and your best years spiritually, physically and financially are ahead of you. Believe that all things are possible to him who believes (Mark 9:23). Your best years are ahead of you!

Jeremiah 29:11 lets us know that God not only has plans for us, but has a hope and a future for us (NKJV). Isaiah 43:18-19 tells us that God does not want us looking back, but only forward since He wants to do new things in our lives. Be encouraged as your best years are ahead of you.

In the next few pages you will read stories of people just like you and me who encountered situations where they were tempted to think and say that it was all over for them. They probably thought their best years were behind them. However, God found them at their lowest and helped them see the glorious future He had for them. Their latter years ended up being the best years of their lives. So if you are in a similar situation as the people you will soon be reading about be encouraged. God still has great plans for you. His mercy endures forever! You have an amazing future!

1

Moses - From Leading Sheep to Leading People

Do not remember the former things, nor consider the things of old. Behold, I will do a new thing, now it shall spring forth.

Isaiah 43:18,19

Let's continue with Moses. If there was ever someone who had it made then lost it all, it was Moses. You will encounter many people in this book who seemingly had it all then lost it. Remember that Egypt was one of the greatest nations in the world at that time and Moses was so near to the throne. It seems that one bad mistake ruined everything.

Don't you think that Moses constantly reminded himself of the Egyptian that he killed, and then continued to beat himself up for it? Remember that he was in the desert for forty years. That is a long time to condemn yourself.

So God appears on the scene and says, "Moses, I have an assignment for you." An assignment means that God is looking at our future not our past. We are looking at it but not God. He not only had an assignment for him but, in essence, a great future. You probably know the rest of the story. The next forty years were the greatest in Moses' one hundred and twenty years.

So where are you in your life, my reader? Are you down looking at a failed marriage, or foreclosure? How about a broken relationship or the rebellion of a son or daughter? I still have to say that your best years are ahead of you, if you determine to continue to believe in the God of the impossible who loves you. Moses had to believe in the God of the impossible because, in the natural, it was impossible to accomplish what God was asking him to do. So do not quit. Keep reading. Your future is bright. Say it, "My future is bright. I have an amazing future because of God's grace!"

2

Joseph - From Papa to Prison

Do not rejoice over me, my enemy; when I fall, I shall arise; when I sit in darkness the Lord will be a light unto me.

Micah 7:8

Another person who seemingly had everything going for him was Joseph. He was his daddy's favorite, he knew it, and so did his brothers. "Hey you want to see my new coat?" he asked, perhaps without understanding how it would make his brothers feel. Did he have to work like his brothers? Probably not.

So he gets thrown into a pit by his jealous brothers and later sold into slavery. Think about this, his own brothers did this to him. He had to go to a different land and learn a new language and new customs. On top of that he had to work. WORK? Hey, I am my father's favorite son he might have thought. This is unfair.

Everyone has experienced at least one act of injustice in their lives. Most have experienced numerous. Life is not always fair. It is not fair to children when parents divorce. Divorce is unfair. The premature death of a loved one is unfair. A soldier's death, rape, sexual abuse at the hands of someone you trusted, even the burglary of your home is unfair. You may be wondering, don't people care? Or perhaps you have even wondered where God was? If there is a God, He must be fair, so why is there so much injustice? Because God IS fair and He has created us with the power of choice or free will.

"But I had no choice in my parents' divorce, the rape or the abuse," you might say. No, you did not, but today you can make a choice on whether you will let it continue to affect you for the rest of your life or determine that the traumatic event will only make you stronger. Where God WAS is not as important as where God is NOW. He is there to empower you with His grace to get up and state, "My best years are ahead of me. I will grow from this mess and with God's help, turn it into a message." Your best years are ahead of you! He loves you with an everlasting love. You have an amazing future!

3

Joseph - From Bad to Worse to Prime Minister

For I know the thoughts I think toward you, says the Lord, thoughts of peace and not of evil, to give you a future and a hope.

Jeremiah 29:11

Let's continue with Joseph. If ever there was a person whose life went from bad to worse it was Joseph. Think about it. He was sold into an Egyptian official's home, worked for him as if he was working for his own future and prosperity, gains the respect of his owner and then gets falsely accused of sexual assault. Everyone has thought at one time or another, "Why is this happening to me when I have committed no wrong and served God and obeyed His commandments?"

So off to prison he went. But, still his best years were ahead of him. He could have thought the best years of his life were with his father. He could have thought he had it made back there. He may have wondered, "Why did I have to be so boastful of my dad's favoritism?" But that still does not justify what his brothers did. Ah, but thank God he did not get bitter and so the best years of his life were ahead of him. He did not know that he was now closer to his dream than ever before. What, in prison? Yes, in prison.

You may be in prison today, literally, but I have to tell you that your best years are ahead of you or the entire Bible is not true. Jeremiah 29:11 states that God has plans for us to give us a future and a hope. You have a future. Joseph had a future. He did not know it, but the best years of his life were ahead of him.

I would like to interject what I heard Creflo Dollar say once. There came a time when Joseph was only thirty days away from becoming Prime Minister of Egypt and he did not even know it. Then there came a time when he was only one day away from becoming Prime Minister and did not know it. Then only one hour away from becoming Prime Minister and did not know it. You see his best years were ahead of him and your best years are ahead of you, too, even though you may not be able to see how in the natural.

The day came when he interpreted Pharaoh's dreams and his own dreams came true. You know the rest of the story. He became Prime Minister of Egypt. So don't quit. Your best years are ahead of you. You have an amazing future!

4

EPHRAIM AND MANASSEH – SO FRUITFUL YOU FORGET

For surely there is a latter end (a future and a reward), and your hope and expectation will not be cut off.

Proverbs 23:18 (AMP)

Joseph eventually became Prime Minister and second in command of the nation of Egypt. As Prime Minister he married and had two sons, Manasseh and Ephraim. Manasseh means causing to forget. His second son was named Ephraim which means fruitful. So what does all this have to do with my amazing future? A lot.

In the course of time Jacob, Joseph's father, knowing he was close to death, called Joseph's two sons to bless them. Jacob, contrary to custom, placed his right hand over the head of Ephraim (the second born) and his left hand over Manasseh (the first born). Joseph corrected his father who in turn corrected Joseph. By placing his right hand over Ephraim, Jacob was declaring a greater blessing over Ephraim than Manasseh. Of course, in those days the first-born received the greater blessing.

Let's see the significance of this. God, through Jacob, was declaring, "I will make you so fruitful (Ephraim) that you will forget your past (Manasseh)." According to the Bible, the Jews actually developed a blessing that they declared over one another stating, "The Lord make you like Ephraim and Manasseh," (Genesis 48:20).

Do you see the beauty here? If you are looking at your past, God wants to make you so fruitful that He will cause you to forget your past. This is something to get excited about. My reader, I declare this over you. "God make you like Ephraim and Manasseh. God make you so fruitful that you forget your past." God is actually empowering us to forget our past by making us so fruitful that He causes us to forget it. Stop now and declare this by faith. "God makes me so fruitful that He causes me to forget my past."

Now get this. He HAS already made us so fruitful we can forget our past. This is the Blessings of Genesis 1:28. Declare that you are (present tense) fruitful and multiplying according to Genesis 1:28. Your best years are ahead of you. You have an amazing future!

5

CALEB – SO CLOSE AND YET SO FAR

The hope (expectation) of the righteous will be gladness...

Proverbs 10:28

Caleb is actually one of my favorite Bible characters. He was not only a great man of vision and faith but he had to have been a man of perseverance as well. Caleb was one of the few adult men (from the group that left Egypt) that actually saw and entered the Promised Land. He actually walked in it, but due to the unbelief of the other spies (except Joshua) he could not get in. However, God promised him that in the future he would get in and stay.

Let's use our imagination for a moment. Don't you think Caleb had a few days when he looked back at the fact that he was actually IN the Promised Land at one time? Think of the fact that he saw the grapes and other fruit that the spies brought back. He actually walked the land and now he was walking with the rest of the nation up and down a deserted land.

On top of this, people probably came up to him year after year (especially the younger crowd) and asked him if it was true that he had seen the Promised Land and walked in it. But he held on to his dream. He was tempted like everyone else, but he refused to look back, get bitter toward the other spies and feel sorry for himself. He kept reminding himself that his future was bright because God had stated that he would make it into the Promised Land and this time stay in it. He reminded himself that his best years were ahead of him and not behind him.

How do I know all this about Caleb? Because a bitter man would not have been able to do what he did at the age of eighty-five. What a testimony to the grace of God when at that age he told Moses that he was as strong as he had been forty-five years prior when he entered the Promised Land for the first time. And then he did it. He conquered the territory that had been promised to him forty-five years earlier. How was he able to do this? Because of God's grace and because he kept telling himself that his best years were ahead of him and this became reality. Like Caleb your best years are ahead of you. You have an amazing future!

A Few Do Not's and Do's on Your Way to Your Amazing Future

Though your beginning was small, yet your latter end would increase abundantly.

Job 8:7

DO NOT:

Look back—We have already discussed this one at length.

Complain—What is there to complain about if you think your best years are ahead of you? Complaining is an excuse to do nothing.

Feel sorry for yourself—When you fall into this one, you believe that others get all the breaks. Stop singing, "Nobody knows the trouble I've seen."

Accept a victim's mentality—Feeling like a victim robs you of your God-given strength, courage and wisdom that you can use to change your life and determine your future.

Hold resentment—This one will keep you stuck in the past more than anything else. Forgive for your own sake. You may not feel like it, but forgiveness is an action not a feeling.

Get into an entitlement mentality—Nobody owes you anything. Stop looking to others to GIVE you a job or a break. Make a break for yourself. People do not GIVE you jobs, you earn them. Breaks are the results of seeds planted, not luck.

DO:

Forgive—This one is worth mentioning again due to its importance. And forgive yourself not just others.

Persevere—Keep dreaming. Stay in faith. Stay in love and keep planting seeds.

Get up if you fall. Someone stated that failure is not in falling, but in not getting up.

See good in every negative situation.

Watch your mouth and watch your thoughts. Death and life are in the power of the tongue. Your life will go in the direction of your most dominant thoughts.

Keep your sense of humor. Can you laugh at yourself?

And above ALL do believe that God loves you and is for you. He loves you greatly. Because His grace is sufficient, you can and will make it. You have an amazing future!

7

JOB

Now the lord blessed the latter days of Job more than his beginning...

Job 42:12

Job is one of the most misunderstood people in the Bible. He was the richest man in the east. He had everything going for him, but through fear he allowed Satan to come in and steal from him. Many are confused about who did what to Job. John 10:10 makes it clear that the devil comes to steal, kill and destroy. So what happened? Well, when God told the devil that Job was in his hands, God was merely pointing out to him that Job had already placed himself in Satan's hands by his fears (Job 3:25). Job's own fears opened himself up to what Satan was able to do in his life.

Job lost it all, got into self-pity, self-righteousness and blaming God. Eventually, he got back into faith when he prayed for his friends (Job 42:7-9) and God ended up restoring double to him (Job 42:10). God gave him seven sons and three daughters and his daughters were the most beautiful in all the land. So you see, God had planned beautiful things for Job's future. Job even lived one hundred and forty years AFTER the calamities in the book of Job, which took no more than a year or so.

So you see that the best years of Job were in front of him when he was going through all the book of Job. He simply did not know it. Thank God that he got back into faith. So, my friend, stay in faith. Resist feeling sorry for yourself and blaming God. You are closer to your breakthrough than you realize. The best years of your life are in front of you just like they were in front of Job when he was IN the mess he was in. Don't give up. God loves you and is for you (Romans 8:31). God can even restore double to you what the devil has stolen. As with Job, God has beautiful things planned for your future because of His grace. You have an amazing future!

8

PETER

Though he fall, he will not be utterly cast down; for the lord upholds him with his hand.

Psalm 37:24

Peter undoubtedly felt that it was all over for him. He had denied Jesus three times. He felt condemned. He might have been able to forgive himself with one denial, but three? And then hearing that Jesus might be alive made it worse. How could he ever face Jesus after all He had done for him?

But then he hears the words sent to him by the women that saw the angel who announced to them to go tell His disciples AND Peter that He wanted to meet with them (Mark 16:7). I can imagine Peter asking the women if the angel had actually mentioned his name personally.

Well, you know the story. He did meet the Master somewhere before the miraculous catch of fish in Chapter

21 of the book of John. We know he had to have had an encounter with Jesus since he swam toward Jesus when John advised him that Jesus was on the shore. If he had not had a previous encounter with Jesus he would have swam the other way.

And then toward the end of Chapter 21 of the book of John, Jesus and Peter have a second encounter and a most intimate conversation. In that conversation Jesus gave a mission to Peter to teach His sheep. This further changed it all for Peter; the Master still had a job for him. He was actually telling Peter, "Peter, you have an amazing future. Your best years are ahead of you. I have a mission for you."

Don't you think that before Jesus restored Peter he spent much time reminding himself of the years in the Sea of Galilee and surrounding areas where he had personally walked and ministered with the Master whom Peter loved? "Ah, yes, those were great years, but now..." Peter must have thought.

But the Master met him in his lowest, restored him and gave him an assignment. No matter what has happened in your life, God's grace is sufficient. He still has a great work for you to do. He did with Peter and He has great things He still wants you to do for Him and others. On top of this, He has great things He wants to do IN you. Again I tell you that your best years are ahead of you. Don't look back, your future is bright. You have an amazing future!

9

JESUS

...Who for the joy (future) that was set before him endured the cross, despising the shame, and has sat down at the right hand of the throne of god.

Hebrews 12:2

Did Jesus ever feel that His best years were behind Him? No. We know this because Hebrews 12:2 states that for the joy that was set before Him He endured the cross. Jesus also stated that He was certain that the Father would not leave His soul in hell (Acts 2:27). Many times Jesus stated in the Gospels that He would die but rise again. He always knew that His best years were ahead of Him.

My friend, our Savior is our champion and our example. If He was able to hold on to the truth that His best years were in front of Him so can we. Remember Jesus operated in the earth as the Son of Man. He put aside

His divinity and lived facing the same temptations that we do and overcame them by grace and faith.

The cross was not the end. Your setback is not the end. Learn from it and grow from it. Jesus has great plans for us. I remember a short time back talking to a young man in prison and telling him that his best years were in front of him and that God had great plans for his life. Even in prison I wanted him to receive these truths because they are truth. I had no problem telling him what I did because the Word of God is still the Word of God even in prison. I am so blessed that he took hold of the words that I shared with him.

Friend, your best years are ahead of you. The best years of the body of Christ are ahead of us. When we have been in eternity for a billion years (yes, I know eternity has no time) we will still be able to state that our best years as the glorious Church are still ahead of us. We will go from glory to glory now and in eternity. Look up. Your best years are ahead of you. You have an amazing future!

10

THE APOSTLE JOHN

The end of a thing is better than its beginning...
Ecclesiastes 7:8

We are all pretty familiar with the life of the Apostle John. In the Book of Revelation he mentions being on the Island of Patmos for "the testimony of Jesus Christ." Remember that John was an older man by then, probably around ninety years old. Patmos, in the natural, was no place for anyone to be, much less a ninety year old man. He was undoubtedly sent there to die. At the least the Emperor who exiled him was hoping to silence the apostle. Of course, he did not. Satan is out to silence our testimony. In the life of the Apostle John it did not work. I believe it will not work in yours either.

Let's imagine the Apostle John landing on the island. In the natural, most of us would have thought that it was all over except the dying part. Knowing human nature, we would have started to question God as to why He was letting us die on the forsaken Island of Patmos. After all, he had served God practically all his life and even cared for the mother of Jesus. Tradition holds that Mary lived with John until her death.

John at the time of his banishment to Patmos was a highly respected elder in the church. He was the only living Apostle of Jesus at that time. Death on Patmos was no place for the "disciple whom Jesus loved" to end his life. Of course, we do not know if these thoughts went through John's mind, but he might have been tempted to think them.

However, Jesus appears to him and tells him that his best was still ahead of him. He added, "I've got an assignment for you, John." Instead of dying on Patmos, John writes the glorious book of Revelation. This book eventually became the last book of the greatest book of all time, the Bible.

So when we think it is over, it is not. When we think God has no more work for us to do, the greatest work is yet to be done. God still has an assignment for you. You are also the disciple that Jesus loves. You have an amazing future!

11

THE PRODIGAL'S FATHER

There is hope in your future, says the lord, that your children shall come back to their own border.

Jeremiah 31:17

When the Lord began to speak to me the simple message that our greatest years were ahead of us He began to place in my spirit to tell people that the greatest years in their relationship with their children were ahead of them. Frankly, we tend to always look back at how our relationships were better when our sons and daughters were younger and living in our home. But if this message is true then lift up your head my friend. Even if you have a wayward child, the best years in your relationship with them is ahead of you.

Let's think of the Prodigal's father. Most of the time we concentrate more on the son than the father. We do not know from the scriptures just how long the son was gone. Maybe it was months or maybe it was years. In any event, the father might have been tempted to think that the best years with his son were behind him. However, if the father of the prodigal paints a picture of our Heavenly Father then we can state that they only got better. Actually, the father's response to the son coming home in running to him, kissing him and honoring his return only indicates the relationship got better.

Think of the prodigal son. He obviously felt that things were never going to be as good as they had once been between him and his father. But, again, I think they got better. What does "where sin abounds grace does much more abound" mean (Romans 5:20)? Also, I love the first phrase in Joel 2:25 where the Lord states, "I will restore the *years*..." When God restores, He never restores to a previous state. He always restores to a better state. Look at the end of the story of Job. God restored double. So we can be assured that the relationship between the father and the son was not only restored but that it got better than it had been before.

So, my friend, be at peace. If you have a son or daughter away from the Lord, call them restored to the Kingdom of God (Isaiah 43:25) and believe that the best years in your relationship with them is ahead of you. You have an amazing future and so do your children!

12

THE WOMAN IN JOHN CHAPTER 8

There is therefore now no condemnation to those who are in Christ Jesus…

Romans 8:1

I am sure if you have read the Bible that you are familiar with the woman caught in the act of adultery by the religious leaders of the day. She was brought to Jesus probably half naked, disheveled and frightened. She probably thought that it was all over for her. The religious leaders cared little for the woman. Their reason in bringing her to Jesus had nothing to do with her and everything to do with wanting to trap Jesus.

The religious leaders asked Jesus what to do with the woman given the fact that the Mosaic law mandated death. If Jesus went contrary to the law then the leaders had something to accuse Jesus of. However, if he agreed with stoning her He would be going against what He had previously stated, that His mission was not to condemn but to save (John 3:16-17). You know what Jesus did so let's concentrate on the woman.

If ever anyone felt that their life was over it was this woman. No one would ever convince her that her best years were ahead of her. But this is exactly what Jesus tells the woman. "Where are your accusers, woman?" He asks. Then he states the greatest, most powerful words the woman could have heard—"Neither do I condemn you." In other words, Jesus just stated to her that her best years were ahead of her.

A few minutes ago she looked at a future where everyone would always identify her as the adulterous woman. Now she has a clean slate. Jesus empowers the woman to avoid further adulterous relationships by releasing her of all condemnation and guilt. The statement, "go and sin no more" was more than just a command to not sin anymore. He was <u>empowering</u> her not to. In other words, He empowered her to not fall into adultery again "looking for love in all the wrong places" by releasing her of all condemnation. Condemnation sets people up to repeat sin. Release from condemnation frees us to "sin no more".

My reader, be released of all condemnation and guilt. Romans 8:1 is clear that there is no condemnation now that we are in Christ. He has forgiven you, now receive it. God is not holding your sins against you (2 Corinthians 5:19) so you are released into a great future. Condemnation keeps you in the past, but you are forgiven and have a great future. Believe this and receive it. You have an amazing future!

13

KING DAVID

You have turned for me my mourning into dancing; you have put off my sackcloth and clothed me with gladness...

Psalm 30:11

If there ever was a person who could be called the "Comeback Kid" it was King David. He came back from numerous defeats in his life. Certainly the death of a child and his own son's rebellion would have destroyed most people. However, he just kept coming back.

His setback at Ziglag at the hands of the Amalekites was one of his greatest setbacks. In 1 Samuel Chapter 30, while David was away, the enemy came and burned the city and took all the women and children captive. Then they stole all they could carry and burned the city. David was in a tight spot since his men cried, the Bible states, until they had no strength left. In a situation like this you usually look for someone to blame. David was it. The men threatened to kill David. However, the Bible states that David strengthened himself in the Lord and sought divine direction.

His question to God is interesting. He states, "Shall I pursue, shall I overtake them?" The Lord responds to David that He should pursue, that he shall surely overtake them AND that he will recover all. Get it? God added to what David asked. This is just like God. David wanted help in <u>pursuing</u> and <u>overtaking</u> them. God said to David that he was not only going to overtake them but recover all. RECOVER ALL. Get it? Recover all of David's stuff and everything else the Amalekites had. And it happened just like God said.

So my friend, PURSUE, OVERTAKE AND RECOVER ALL of whatever has been stolen by the devil, whether it be it health, finances or relationships. Spend time with God as David did and God will give you directions step by step. Take it one step at a time. And if in your pursuit obstacles occur keep moving forward. David had one third of his men quit due to exhaustion but he kept pursuing, overtook and recovered all. And so will you. He loves you and is for you. You have an amazing future!

14

Finish Your Race

I have fought a good fight, I have finished the race, I have kept the faith.

2 Timothy 4:7

What a great phrase, "I have finished my race, I have kept the faith." These were the Apostle Paul's great words toward the end of his life. Our Master Himself stated on the cross, "It is finished." In discussing your amazing future, it is important to finish what God sent you to earth to do. God has made us more than conquerors and that makes us finishers.

I remember as a young boy hearing a guest speaker in our church tell us about a race that he was involved in. He did not win. In fact, he came in if not last one of the last. He was surprised to hear his name called after the winners had been given their trophies. He thought he was hearing incorrectly but still went up to the podium. To his surprise he was given an award for finishing.

Of course, as Christians we not only want to finish, but finish strong. In Jesus' name we will. Only in believing that our greatest years are ahead of us can we finish strong. We were created to go from glory to glory and from victory to victory. Discover, develop and deploy what God sent you to earth to do.

Remember that David was called a man after God's own heart. Why? One reason was because, even in the Old Testament, David had a revelation of grace. See how in Psalm 32:2 he talks about the blessedness of the man to whom the Lord would not impute iniquity. He was looking into the future where today God does not impute iniquity unto us since all our sins were placed on Jesus.

This belief helped David finish all God called him to do. He even wanted to build the temple, but God said no. Therefore, David prepared and gave billions (in today's economy) for the project that his son was to start and finish.

Get a hold of this. A righteous man's works follow him after his death. Could we say that David's greatest work (the funding of the temple) followed him after his death? Yes, he had an amazing future. Do not leave earth until you are finished, until you finish all the amazing things God sent you to earth to accomplish. You can with God's grace. Your own works done for God's glory will follow you after you leave earth if the Lord tarries. You have an amazing future!

15

Your Best Years Are Ahead of You

So I will restore to you the years that the swarming locust has eaten...

Joel 2:25

Have you been standing believing God for the restoration of your marriage? Then don't quit because the best years of your marriage are ahead of you. Continue to speak the Word of God over your marriage. It is no coincidence that Jesus' first miracle was in a marriage feast. Marriages are important to Him. As he did in the marriage at Cana (John 2) He can turn the water in your marriage into wine.

> He turned the water into wine
>
> He turned the water into wine
>
> He'll turn your scars into stars

> Your pain into gain
>
> He turned the water into wine
>
> © Samuel Martinez

Are you standing for healing? Believe that the best years of your health are ahead of you. As I mentioned previously, God stated in Joel 2:25 that He would restore the years.

Have years been robbed through debilitating illness? God wants to restore the years. Are you a tither and giver? Continue to believe for the return on your giving because your best years financially are ahead of you. But, Samuel, I am now on a fixed income. However, in the kingdom of God there is no such thing as a fixed or limited income. Our income is only limited to the extent that we stop giving or we stop believing God for the return on our sowing.

I want to state again that the best years of your life are ahead of you. Review the Bible verses noted in the book. Nothing will motivate you more than reading Bible verses on your amazing future. Do the confession of faith at the end of the book and believe that your greatest years are ahead of you. You have an amazing future because God loves you and is for you. He is not holding your past sins or mistakes against you. You have an amazing future!

16

WHAT MORE SHALL I SAY?

Taking a line from Hebrews 11:32, what more shall I say for the time would fail me to talk of so many who accomplished great things in their latter years and those who overcame defeats. Even Samson when He had his eyes gouged out did not know that he had a great future. Yes, I know that he died in his last feat, but it was still his greatest feat. What a way to go!

And what of people like Grandma Moses who was "discovered" at the age of eighty. Her first paintings sold for $5.00, but in 2006 a painting of hers sold for over a million dollars. It bears mentioning that at the age of seventy-six she developed arthritis so she could no longer take up embroidery. Hence, she started painting. She could have gotten bitter over her inability to do embroidery, but instead her scars were turned to stars.

What of Harry Bernstein who for seven decades had over forty novels rejected, but at ninety-three published his memoir "The Invisible Wall." I love his quote, "If I had not lived until I was ninety, I would not have been able to write this book, God knows what other potentials lurk in other people, if we could only keep them alive well into their 90's."

I also love the quote from Nola (Hill) Ochs who remarked, "It's been the Lord's will that I've lived this long life, and I thank Him kindly for it." Nola received a Master's Degree from Fort Hays State University at the age of ninety-eight.

Yes, it is God's will that we live a long life and that we comeback from all setbacks in life. Jesus came back and so can you. You have an amazing future!

17

The Birth of Modern Israel

For I will take you from among the nations, gather you out of all countries, and bring you into your own land.

Ezekiel 36:24

On May 14, 1948 David Ben-Gurion chairman of the Jewish Agency proclaimed the State of Israel, establishing the first Jewish state in 2000 years. He declared, "we hereby proclaim the establishment of the Jewish state in Palestine to be called Israel." The United States recognized the new nation. At midnight the Jewish state officially came into existence. On the next day, Israel was attacked by several Arab nations. Though the Arab armies were well equipped and Israel had no regular army, Israel survived. Through the years, Israel has had to fight for its existence but it has prevailed.

The present nation of Israel is a testimony to the integrity of the Word of God. Though Israel had been judged for their idolatries and scattered throughout the earth, God had promised to bring them back to the land He had promised them in the Old Testament.

I can only imagine the Jewish people, century after century, wondering when the promises of God were going to be fulfilled, especially after the horrific holocaust. The people of God were even admonished in Psalm 137 not to forget Jerusalem. In 1967 after the Six Day War, old Jerusalem came into the hands of the new nation. Psalm 137:6 states, "if I do not remember you, let my mouth cling to the roof of my mouth—If I do not exalt Jerusalem above my chief joy."

On top of this is the mention in Isaiah 35:1 that the desert would blossom as the rose. Israel through their ingenuity in technology and irrigation has restored a parched land into a fertile and productive land. However, Israel still has its best years ahead of it. As amazing as the birth of modern Israel has been and the desert blossoming when Messiah returns, more scriptures on Israel's prophesized amazing future will be fulfilled.

And yet, no matter what difficulties you may be going through today, you can obtain great encouragement every time you think of the nation of Israel. Israel has an amazing future and so do you. Do not let go of the promises of God. Roses will bloom in your desert. Roses will bloom again. You (and Israel) have an amazing future.

18

THE TWO MEN ON THE ROAD TO EMMAUS

"Did not our hearts burn within us while He talked with us on the road, and while He opened the scriptures to us?"

Luke 24:32

You can hear the disappointment in the hearts of these two men as they talked with Jesus, unaware they were talking to the risen Savior. In Luke 24 verses 19 to 20, they share with our Savior about a man named Jesus who was, "mighty in word and deed" but was tragically crucified by the religious leaders. Verse 21 states, "We were hoping that it was He who was to redeem Israel." In the four words "But we were hoping" you can hear the discouragement, the disappointment and the pain in the hearts of the men.

Ah, but the Savior opened up the Word to them that the sufferings of the Messiah were prophesied and as He took bread, blessed it and gave it to them, their eyes were opened. Of course, you know Jesus immediately vanished from their sight, since it was more important to Jesus that they see Him in the Word than physically. They themselves stated that their hearts burned within them as He opened up the scriptures to them.

In the middle of the night, they returned several miles to Jerusalem from where they were coming when Jesus encountered them. They found the 11 disciples and shared that Jesus was alive. All hope that had been lost was restored, not just because Jesus was alive, but because they now understood the scriptures that Jesus had opened up to them. Hope was restored and disappointment vanished, not just because they saw Jesus (of course this was a great part of their joy) but because the Word had been opened up to them.

My friends, joy does not come when the circumstances change but when the Word of the Lord is opened up to us. The disciples, before Jesus encountered them, did not know that they had a great future ahead of them. Walking from Jerusalem to Emmaus, they did not realize that their whole lives were about to change as the Word was opened unto them.

In the same manner God has an amazing future planned for us. Every day as we spend time in the Word, we have it opened unto us by the Holy Spirit. As we see Jesus in the Word, we are tapping into our amazing future. It is in beholding Jesus in the Word that you are transformed from discouragement and loss of hope to realizing that you have an amazing future.

19

THE PEOPLE TOUCHED BY JESUS' MIRACLES

How God anointed Jesus of Nazareth with the Holy Spirit and with power, who went about doing good and healing all who were oppressed by the devil, for God was with Him.

Acts 10:38

In this chapter let us focus on the many people who were touched by Jesus' miracles. The book of John states that all the books in the world could not contain all the miracles of Jesus if they were to be written. It is amazing the number of people Jesus touched in his 3 year plus ministry on the earth.

Think of the woman with the issue of blood. Until she heard of Jesus she thought it was all over for her, and in the natural, it was. What about Jairus hearing that his daughter was dead? He was tempted to believe that it was all over or Jesus would not have encouraged him to "believe only." The blind, the deaf and maimed could not imagine a future that was bright and vibrant, but as a song I heard as a young man states, "but Jesus came" and, of course, everything changed. They did not know that they had an amazing future. Jesus raised more than one person from the dead. In physical death, many think it is definitely all over. But Jesus came and their future changed.

This short book has been about people who had setbacks, thought it was over but actually had an amazing future. The Bible does not state much of what happened to the people who Jesus healed, raised from the dead or delivered. But we can imagine the amazing future they had. Even if they had had a great life before their illness or whatever other setback occurred, life became greater.

It has been said that one word from God can change your life forever. Of course, we also know that one encounter with Jesus can change one's life forever. I believe that this is a great thing that our Savior relished doing—changing the direction of people's lives forever. Of course, when the spiritual life of another is changed, it is for eternity. Nonetheless, Jesus does not make a difference between our spiritual needs and physical ones. They are both important to Him.

I can tell you with certainty that the people whose lives were changed by Jesus ministering to their physical needs followed Jesus in their hearts for the rest of their lives. It was not just the physical benefits that changed the people but the compassion of our Savior. Think for a minute the compassion that changed the leper forever when Jesus <u>touched</u> him and told him he was more than willing to heal him.

This is what all the people in this book and in the Bible encountered—the compassion of the Lord. This is what changes people. Encounter His love, my reader. He loves you and wants you to know that because of Him you have an amazing future.

20

WOMAN AT THE WELL, JOHN CHAPTER FOUR

"Come see a man who told me all things I ever did."

John 4:29

The woman at the well is somewhat unlike some of the other people in this book. She was not imprisoned like Joseph nor was rejected like Moses. In a sense, however, she is like these two because although she was not imprisoned physically, she was emotionally. Unlike Moses, she was not rejected for leadership by her people, but undoubtedly felt rejected by the other women in her village. That is the reason she came to draw water at noon when most people came before it got too hot.

After five husbands, she felt that the dream of finding someone of the opposite sex to value her was over. But along came someone of the opposite sex, our Savior, who told her things about herself that a stranger would not know and communicated value to her. Many times in life it is not so much what we say, but from what heart it is coming.

What Jesus shared with her came from a caring heart. But before He told her things about herself that a stranger would not know, He asks her for a drink of water. This was significant because Jesus told her, in essence, that He needed something from her. As He asked for a drink of water, which surprised her, Jesus was able to draw the conversation to what He needed from her.

Listen, my readers. So many times we come to Jesus to ask what we can do for <u>Him</u> and He just wants us to receive what He has for <u>us</u>. He had living water that He wanted to give her if she was willing to receive. Our Father is looking for receivers more than achievers. Of course, we want to do for Him, and so we should, but God wants us first of all to daily receive His love, as well as His mercy and grace. Note how Paul starts almost of all his letters with the greeting of grace and peace. In other letters he adds mercy. It is as if the first thing God wants us to receive from Him as we approach His word, and start every day, is His grace, mercy and peace.

The woman's life that day was changed because she stopped to receive what Jesus had for her. The very fact that Jesus even talked to her communicated value. The Bible leaves silent what happened to the woman after her ONE DAY encounter with Jesus, but I believe her future became bright. Rejection and shame were eliminated from her life. She had an amazing future and so do you.

21

The Value of One, The Found Sheep

And when he has found it, he lays it on his shoulders rejoicing.

Luke 15:5

The parable of the lost sheep should really be the parable of the found sheep. In this parable our Savior is painting a picture of His love for us. He is truly the Great Shepherd. Although this is a book about people who have setbacks and came back, let's focus on the sheep because it is all about us.

Somehow I had always assumed that the lost sheep purposely left the sheepfold and got lost through wrong decisions. But Luke really does not paint a picture of a rebellious sheep, although the sheep may have been stubborn. The point is, that for whatever reason the sheep got <u>lost</u>. I have seen pictures of the lonely sheep close to a cliff probably cold and hungry. Though I am not sure of the mental acumen of sheep, let's imagine for a moment (since this is a story about us) that the sheep probably thought it was all over. It may have imagined falling off the cliff or even becoming someone's dinner. The Bible does not state this, but it could have been lost for a few hours or a whole day.

Now let's focus on the actions of our hero, the Shepherd. He left the ninety-nine and went looking for the lost sheep until He found it. Furthermore, when He found the sheep did He beat it? Of course not! The Bible states that He laid it on his shoulders and returned it to the fold rejoicing.

It is quite interesting to me that the parable ends by Jesus stating that in the same manner there is more joy in heaven over one sinner who repents than ninety-nine who need no repentance. So did the sheep repent? And what did the sheep repent of? The sheep repented by consenting to be rescued and carried home. Repentance is really a change of mind. The sheep (stay with me here) could have felt unworthy of all the efforts of the hero shepherd and rejected his help. Farfetched? Not really. Remember this is really a story about us. How many times do we reject the help of our Shepherd by feeling condemned and guilty over our actions? Remember the previous chapter where it was discussed how it is so important to God that we receive from Him?

I believe the sheep returned to the sheepfold and refused to feel condemned for having to be rescued. I believe the sheep had a great future and so will you. Consent to be loved and carried. He loves you. You have an amazing Shepherd and amazing future.

22

THE APOSTLE PAUL

I have fought the good fight, I have finished the race, I have kept the faith.

2 Timothy 4:7

The Apostle Paul wrote most of the New Testament, and among scholars is looked upon as the greatest exponent of the Christian faith. There are so many revelations that he has brought to the body of Christ, such as the authority of the believer. But the apostle had setbacks like everybody else. After his conversion, the book of Acts indicates that he immediately began to preach that Christ was the Son of God. But the ninth chapter of Acts also indicates that when he tried to join forces with the disciples in Jerusalem they were afraid of him. After some coaxing by Barnabas, the disciples initially accepted Paul, but when his boldness in preaching brought an attempt on his life the disciples apparently felt Paul was too much trouble to have around. The solution was to send him back to Tarsus, his home town.

Now think for a minute. Paul had a glorious conversion. He wanted to preach and undoubtedly continued preaching in Tarsus. However, in the natural his ministry would have had a greater impact in Jerusalem and in the company of the other leaders of the church. But the other leaders did not see it that way. Not much is known about Paul's reaction to the decision to send him back to Tarsus, but he could have seen this action as a step back when he had left all he had built in his resume (see Philippians chapter 3:5-8) to follow Jesus.

And what about his stoning in Acts 14:19 that left him almost dead? He was dragged out of town after the stoning yet got back up and returned to the same city he was stoned in to continue preaching. Later he had another supposed setback when imprisoned for freeing a demon oppressed girl. However, in prison he started a revival.

All this brings us to Acts 27, when on his way to Rome Paul encountered a hurricane and in his own words "all hope that we would be saved was finally given up." Note the word "we." However, Paul had a word from the Lord that he would preach in Rome (Acts 23:11) and was rescued even when all hope was lost. Paul made it to Rome and the book of Acts concludes with the statements that for the next two years Paul preached the gospel with no one "forbidding him." Listen to me as I conclude this chapter. Paul had lost hope in the midst of the hurricane, unaware that he had an amazing future waiting for him in Rome.

Imagine what the Apostle Paul was able to accomplish for the Kingdom of God in those two years. Some may focus on the fact that he probably was martyred in Rome, but why focus on this and not the two years of what was undoubtedly glorious preaching? In the midst of the hurricane he had an amazing future and in the midst of what you may be going through you have an amazing future as you do what Paul did in Acts 27:25 when the angel appeared and told him of his deliverance. He simply stated… "I believe God that it will be just as it was told me".

Believe God that it will be just as the scriptures that were mentioned at the start of each chapter said. I will mention four final things Paul did or said in Acts 27. He stood up (verse 21), took heart (verse 22), and reminded himself to Whom, he belonged and Whom he served (verse 23). **Stand up, my friend, take heart and remember Who you belong to, Who you serve and that your Heavenly Father loves you.** Paul had an amazing future waiting for him in the midst of the storm and so do you. Take heart! He loves you. You have an amazing future!

23

ABSENT FROM THE BODY

Absent from the body...present with the Lord.
2 Corinthians 5:8

In the last chapter I mentioned that the last two years of Paul's life were spent preaching unhindered the word of God in Rome. I also mentioned that he was probably martyred there. Again why center in on his death there and not the two years of glorious preaching with signs and wonders following? Paul never just simply preached the Word of God. God confirmed his preaching with signs and wonders.

In this chapter I want to center in what most Christians do not like to talk about much—our death or our departure from our body. Paul died as a martyr, but the word of God states in Hebrews 2:9 that Jesus tasted death for all of us. Therefore, if we believe this scripture we will not taste death in the sense of death being painful for us.

This same Paul stated that to be absent from the body was to be present with the Lord (2 Corinthians 5:6). So even in dying we have an amazing future. Absent from the body means the instant we leave our body we will be with the Lord. That very instant. To say that very second is too long. It will be as in the twinkling of an eye.

I had to have surgery once and was placed under anesthesia. I really felt nothing until I woke up. Then when I awoke I felt something that was not too pleasant. But in dying there is nothing to fear when we leave, and when we find ourselves with Jesus, we will feel only joy unspeakable and full of glory.

Paul had no fear of dying. In fact, he points out in Philippians that he really preferred to leave and be with Jesus, which he called, "far better." We sing many songs about heaven and seeing Jesus, but no one seems to have the desire Paul had of leaving. Do not get me wrong. Do not leave until you can say as Paul did before he died that he had accomplished what God gave him to do.

My point again is that even in death we have an amazing future. Too amazing to describe in human words. No, don't leave until you are done. However, do not fear death. Paul's words in 1 Corinthians were the words of victory:

Death is swallowed up in victory. O Death where is your sting? But thanks be to God who gives us the victory through our Lord Jesus Christ (2 Corinthians 15:54,55,57).

So again I say, even in death, we have an amazing future so we have nothing to fear. If we stay we have an amazing future. If we leave we have an amazing future. We never lose. You have an amazing future.

24

ELIJAH AND THE WIDOW

And Elijah said to her, "Do not fear;...but make me a small cake from it first and bring it to me..."

1 Kings 17:13

The widow in 1 Kings 17 undoubtedly felt that it was all over for her and her son. There was a drought in the land and food was scarce. In the midst of her despair, a seemingly insensitive and self-centered prophet shows up and asks her for a morsel of bread. What audacity of the man of God! But God had a future for the prophet and the widow.

When asked for the bread her response indicates her present state of hopelessness. She relates to the prophet that she has only a little bit of flour and oil and is going to prepare something for herself and her son, then die. Wow! She tells the prophet exactly what she has in her future and who she sees in her future and that Elijah is not included in it. This woman is adamant!

Ah, but she had an amazing future and did not know it. She had supernatural abundance in her future. She has life and not death for her and her son in her future. According to scripture, the drought lasted three and a half years (James 5:17). Think about it, a three and a half years return on a seed of one morsel of bread. But that is not all! The prophet ate as well and we all know prophets like to eat.

So get this picture. The prophet shows up with miracles of provision and life from the Lord and the woman did not know it. What great things God has in store for our future and we do not know it! Remember, Jeremiah 29:11 and Ephesians 2:10, where God points to our amazing future. He points to the great things He has already planned for us to enjoy. God did it for the widow and her son. He had already planned an amazing future for her; He just needed her trust in Him through the man of God.

That is all God needs from us-our trust. But it should be noted in this brief biblical story that she did not trust or act until she heard a word from the Lord. The prophet told her that the word of the Lord was that her flour and oil would not run out until rain returned. It was only then that she gave.

If you are having problems trusting God, return to the scriptures noted in previous chapters and mediate on them. You do not need a word from the Lord given by a prophet. We now have the written Word, which is greater. Believe He loves you. In the midst of the famine and pending death of her son, she had an amazing future and so do you!

25

ELISHA AND THE WIDOW

"Go, borrow vessels from everywhere, from all your neighbors…"

2 Kings 4:5

Elisha, who followed Elijah, had his own encounter with a widow. Obviously God loves widows. Widows in a larger sense represent all that feel alone, without the help and resources to make it in life. Perhaps no one feels more alone and helpless than widows or single parents. However, there is hope and help from a great and loving Father.

As Elisha encounters the widow in Second Kings chapter 4 she is broke and is about to lose her sons into slavery due to her debts. You can only imagine the pain of a mother about to lose her children. One of the greatest fears of widows and single parents is what is going to happen to their children now that they have to raise them by themselves. I believe God brought Elisha to help the woman concerning her physical needs, but perhaps also to serve as a male role model to her sons. Single parents, you are not alone. Believe God to bring godly men and women around you to help you raise them in the Lord. Believe for His grace and wisdom to parent every day.

Well, you probably know the story. God miraculously multiplied the one jar of oil that the woman had and she in essence "struck oil." She had so much oil that she started selling the oil. The scripture states that she was able to pay her debts and "lived on the rest" (2 Kings 4:7). The implication seems to be that she lived on the rest of the oil for the rest of her life or at least for some extended period of time. But when the oil stopped flowing in the story did the provision stop? I don't know. Maybe she invested properly and even when the oil ran out she had managed her resources to be set for a long time.

My point is that when she cried out in desperation to Elisha God already had an amazing future planned for her. Likewise widows, single parents, orphans or anyone finding yourselves alone and with an insurmountable problem, God has already planned an amazing future for you. Do as the widow did. Listen to the Lord's directions even when they do not seem logical. This widow went to her neighbors to ask for vessels. Imagine being asked what she wanted the vessels for and having to explain her scarcity of oil.

Follow His directions to your amazing future. You are not alone. You have an amazing future!

26

THE BLIND MAN OF JOHN CHAPTER NINE

And Jesus said, "For judgment I have come into this world, that those who do not see may see…"

John 9:39

In a previous chapter I wrote about all the people Jesus healed and how they were changed by His compassion displayed in His power. In this chapter, however, I want us to discuss the man born blind mentioned in John chapter 9. All of Jesus' miracles were great, but this one stands out in my mind because He was born blind, which is unique in and of itself. However, this miracle is also unique because of the setbacks he encountered <u>after</u> he was healed.

I can imagine the man who had to be lowered through the roof having an amazing future. He was forgiven <u>and</u> healed. The woman with the issue of blood was not only healed, but her relationships, impacted by her illness, were restored. Additionally, her finances, I believe, were restored as well because of what Jesus stated at the end of the encounter. He told her "Go in peace and be healed of your affliction" (Mark 4:34). Jesus would have been talking to her in Hebrew and said to go in shalom. Shalom means wholeness, nothing missing and nothing broken. A well-known Bible teacher states that in the Greek Jesus told her to go <u>into</u> peace.

But unlike the others, Jesus healed this man who suffered rejection from his parents and the religious leaders after being healed. The man may have thought how wonderful it was to be able to see, but not understand why perhaps the most important people in his life were not rejoicing along with him. Likewise, perhaps you have had an encounter with Jesus and can't understand people not rejoicing with you and even rejecting you. Ah, but your future is about to get even brighter. I will tell you how the blind man's future got even better later.

First, let's review that his parents practically disowned him due to fearing the religious leaders. The leaders had stated that anyone that confessed that Jesus was the Christ would be cast out of the synagogue. Later in this story, the religious leaders cast this man out of the synagogue. My margin states that they excommunicated him. So think about it. This poor man, blind all his life, is now healed and his parents are ashamed of him and the religious leaders want nothing to do with him. Not a nice picture.

Ah, but he had an even greater future ahead of him than what he thought. But what could be greater than having his eyes opened? Having his spiritual eyes opened! You see, Jesus did not reveal Himself as the Son of God, as the Christ, to just a few. Jesus heard what had happened to the man, encountered him and revealed to him that He was the Christ. Once this happened, I am sure, that the man forgot about the rejection of his parents and the religious leaders. He now knew something few people actually knew. On top of that, he got to worship Jesus.

So if you have suffered rejection due to your stand for Jesus, or other reasons, believe that you have an amazing future and that your past does not dictate your future. Jesus dictates your future. Get in the Word and see Jesus in it. See His great love for you, that in Him you have been made the very righteousness of God in Christ and that as He is so are you in this world (1 John 4:17). When God looks at you, He sees Jesus, and sees you holy and without blame (Ephesians 1:4). The former blind man saw Jesus, in the natural, but in the Word our spiritual eyes are opened and we can behold the beauty of Jesus. And when we discover in the Word the beauty of Jesus, we discover our beauty in Him. Yes, you have an amazing future!

27

HE LIFTS YOU UP

But you, O Lord are a shield for me, my glory, and the lifter of my head.

Psalm 3:3

In John 15:3 Jesus stated that, "Every branch in Me that does not produce fruit He (the Father) will take away." However, my margin states that the last phrase, "He takes away," can also be translated "lifts up." This changes the entire meaning of the verse. Think about this for a minute. From what we have learned about Jesus does the first rendition sound like our Savior?

The Greek word "airo" has a primary meaning of "to lift up." "To take away" is its secondary meaning. Remember what the shepherd did with the lost sheep? He lifted it up and carried it on his shoulders. Furthermore, the word "prunes" in the next line should be "cleans." The word "prunes" in the Greek is "kathairo," which comes from the word translated "clean" in verse 3. So this verse could be translated in this way, "every branch in me that does not produce fruit He lifts up and every branch that bears fruit He cleans so that it can bear more fruit." Then verse three tells us how God cleans us, by His Word.

Vine branches on the ground will not produce fruit. They need to be lifted up on a trellis. So let God lift you up. Stop trying to make it on your own. Stop trying to get yourself out of the mess you may have gotten yourself into through your own bad decisions. Let him lift you up as you get into the Word. Do not stay away from Bible studies or fellowship with other Christians. Do not think of returning to church when you are doing better or have overcome whatever brought you down. Remember that He is good and His mercy endures forever.

Let God lift you up daily. Receive His love everyday by reminding yourself that you are loved, that you are forgiven and that you are the righteousness of God in Christ. He is in you (1 John 4:4), for you (Romans 8:31) and on your side (Psalm 118:6).

In Jeremiah 33:4-10, we have great promises of restoration. Verse 6 speaks of healing, verse 7 of release to the captives, verse 8 of the forgiveness of sins, verse 9 of goodness and prosperity, and verses 10-11 of joy and gladness. Verse 11 concludes that when God brings restoration there will be heard again the voice of those who declare, "Praise the Lord of hosts, For the Lord is good, For His mercy endures forever."

One way God lifts us up is through His Word. Another powerful way is through lifting up our voices and declaring that the Lord is good and His mercy endures forever. Do it, my friend and you will be lifted up. Don't wait till you feel better. He loves you and is on your side. Restoration will occur because you have an amazing future!

Epilogue to Pastors and Others

Pastors, the best days of your church and ministry are ahead of you. God wants you to finish strong. Even if there have been setbacks, keep believing that the Lord has great plans for your church and ministry.

Businessmen, the best days of your businesses are ahead of you. Even if there have been setbacks in your business, cutbacks, layoffs and the like, if you are doing what God has told you to do then your best days are ahead of your business. Remember that the economy does not determine the success of your business. Your faith, integrity and sowing determine the success of your business.

Have you suffered the death of a loved one? Perhaps your spouse of many years has gone on to heaven or a child has departed. Well, rest assured that Jesus bore the chastisement of your peace so His peace would be with you. I speak peace to you. It is not just a catchy phrase to say that they are in a much better place and that you will be with them for all eternity. Therefore, allow me to say that the best years with your loved ones are still ahead of you.

And for all you patriots, America's greatest years are still ahead of her. In other words, God is not through with America. Do not join the preachers of doom. America has yet to see her finest hour. The greatest revival America has ever had is still to come. And when it shows up join it and say, "Glory to God this is great BUT America's and my greatest hour is still to come." God never peaks.

I like baseball. I have mentioned many times that baseball players peak. No matter how good a player is, after a while (unless he is on steroids) his greatest years are behind him. But the Christian life is not a baseball game. We will never peak, but just go from glory to glory (2 Corinthians 4:16).

Wherever there are setbacks the wisdom of God is available. This alone should encourage us. In James 1:2-5 the Bible encourages us that if any man - that means **<u>ANY man</u>** lacks wisdom (in the midst of a trial) God is there to provide it. If our future was not bright why would the Spirit tell us that God wants to give wisdom to all men in the midst of trials? He gives us wisdom to recover and wisdom to go beyond where we were when the setback came. Be encouraged your future is bright. Your best years are still ahead of you. You have an amazing future!

Confession for Your Future

Father, I thank You in Jesus' name that I have a great future. My best years are still ahead of me. The best years of my marriage, my relationships, my ministry and my best years physically are still before me. My best years financially are still to come. I see by faith into my future and I call it bright. My path is like the shining sun that shines ever brighter unto the perfect day.

Ephesians 2:10 (Amplified Bible) states that You prepared ahead of time paths for me to walk in leading to the good life which You prearranged and made ready for me to live. Father, thank You for the plans that You have for me. Plans to give me a future and a hope.

My strength is being renewed like the eagles. Like Isaac, I have begun to prosper, will continue prospering and become very prosperous. I am going from glory to glory, from victory to victory and from faith to faith. I shall finish my race, keep the faith and finish strong in Jesus' name. Because of Your grace and love for me I have an amazing future!

Quotations on Your Future

Don't look back. Something might be gaining on you.

– Satchel Paige

The past is the past so let it pass.

– Samuel Martinez

Your future is so bright you need sunglasses to look at it.

– Joyce Meyers

Forgive, forget and be free.

– Anonymous

Recognize that you will spend much of your time making mistakes. If you can take action and keep making mistakes you gain experience.

– John Maxwell

The past is a place of reference not residence.

– Anonymous

The secret of your future is hidden in your daily routines.

— Mike Murdock

The only time you should look back is to give God praise for what He has brought you through and to.

— Samuel Martinez

There are better days ahead than any we leave behind

— C.S. Lewis

And God will wipe away every tear from their eyes; there shall be no more death, nor sorrow, nor crying; and there shall be no more pain, for the former things have passed away

— Revelation 21:4

Psalms, Hymns, and Spiritual Songs

HE WILL NEVER LET GO OF YOUR HAND

He will never, never let go of your hand,
He will never, never let go of your hand,
Though the rains may come (and they will)
Every now and then,
He will never, never let go of your hand.

He will never, never stop loving you,
He will never, never stop loving you,
His love is everlasting, it endures forever,
He will never, never stop loving you.

HE TURNED THE WATER INTO WINE

He turned the water into wine,

He turned the water into wine,

He'll turn your scars into stars,

Your pain into gain,

He turned the water into wine.

HIS MERCIES ARE NEW

His mercies are new, yes His mercies are new,

His mercies are new every morning,

As fresh as the dew and they're just for you,

His mercies are new every morning.

ROSES WILL BLOOM AGAIN

Roses will bloom again, roses will bloom again,
You may be down, but it is only the first round,
You will be up again.

Roses will bloom; showers will fall upon the incorruptible seed.
Bring forth your goal, so go for the gold,
For roses will bloom again.

Roses will bloom again, roses will bloom again,
Keep on casting your bread upon the waters,
It will come back to you.

Roses will bloom; showers will fall upon the incorruptible seed.
Bring forth your goal, so go for the gold,
For roses will bloom again.

ALL SONGS© SAMUEL MARTINEZ

Amazing Love Ministries

Amazing Love Ministries (formerly Christian Faith Center) was established in 2001. We are a non denominational and bilingual church, part of the FCF fellowship of churches.

Our pastor's life changed in 1975 when as a young man he discovered John 14:12, indicating that the age of miracles and signs and wonders had never ceased.

Our vision is to proclaim the love and the goodness of God to a lost and dying world and equip the saints to do the works of Jesus.

Pastor Samuel Martinez was ordained in 1986. He teaches with humor and clarity the love of God, who we are in Christ Jesus and our authority as believers.

All contact information is listed here:

Email: Smartinez@cfaith.com

Correspondence:
Amazing Love Ministries
216 S. Citrus
P O Box 503
West Covina, CA 91791

About the Author

Samuel Martinez was ordained in 1986 and has been a full-time pastor since 2001. Prior to his work in the ministry, he served in the counseling field, with a master's degree in Marriage, Family and Child Counseling. Pastor Martinez's church offers both English and Spanish services, and his favorite themes to teach include the love and goodness of God. Pastor Martinez and his wife have been married over 45 years.

www.ingramcontent.com/pod-product-compliance
Lightning Source LLC
Chambersburg PA
CBHW050507120526
44588CB00044B/1669